draw Groovy

kids DIY

Thaneeya McArdle

IMPACT
CINCINNATI, OHIO
impact-books.com

Contents

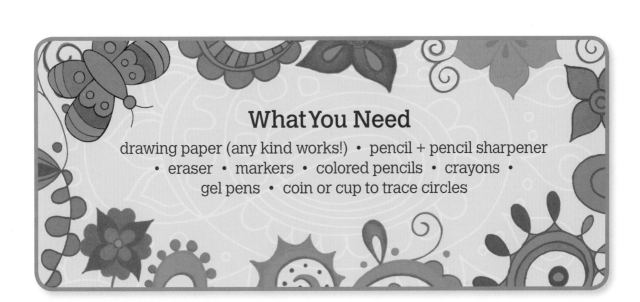

What You Need

drawing paper (any kind works!) • pencil + pencil sharpener
• eraser • markers • colored pencils • crayons •
gel pens • coin or cup to trace circles

This book shows you how to draw fun groovy art that is full of color and style. The best thing about drawing groovy? There are NO RULES! When you draw groovy, you can let your imagination take over and draw the world the way YOU want to see it. Let loose and express yourself!

When you follow these lessons, remember that you *don't* have to copy each step in this book exactly. You can change the colors, choose different shapes and create your own patterns. The possibilities are endless, so you can draw the lessons in this book over and over again, making them different each time. Each drawing can be as unique as you want it to be. Experiment and *have fun*!

Introduction

Drawing Materials

When you follow the lessons in this book, you can use whatever drawing supplies you have on hand. Here are some of the different supplies you can use to create your groovy drawings. Take note of how each type of drawing utensil leaves a different type of mark.

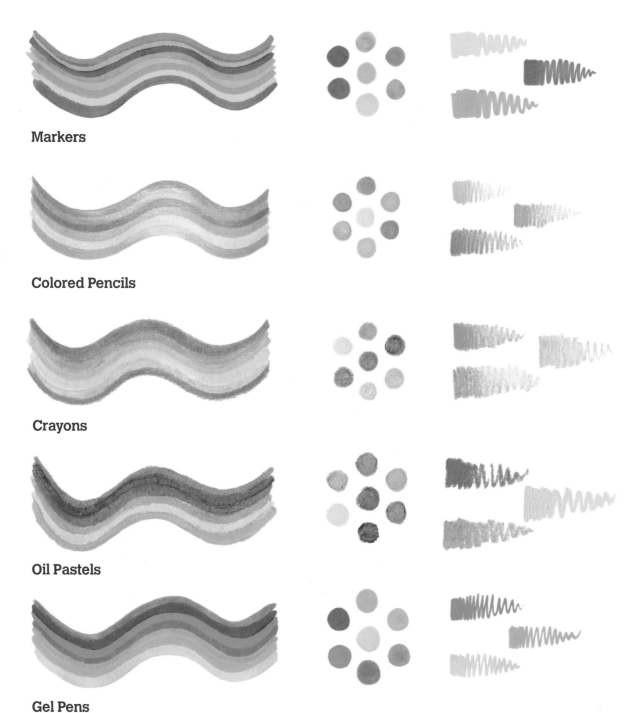

Markers

Colored Pencils

Crayons

Oil Pastels

Gel Pens

Basic Drawing Process

The lessons in this book alternate between two types of drawing processes, drawing with pencil first then coloring, or coloring right from the start. Which way is better? It depends on the lesson and your personal preference. It's really up to you! Sometimes it's easier to draw in pencil first, and sometimes it just adds an extra step you don't really need. Try drawing both ways and see which you prefer.

Pencil First Then Coloring

One way to create groovy drawings is to start with a light pencil drawing so you can erase mistakes, then add color with markers, colored pencils or other coloring tools. This process takes a bit more patience, but it helps you learn to plan your drawings, and it all pays off in the end when it's time to color!

Coloring From the Start

You can draw with color right from the start using markers, colored pencils or other coloring tools in your drawing as you go. This process appeals to people who like to jump right in and create art, but the downside is that it can be hard (or impossible) to erase or cover up mistakes when they happen.

Basic Shapes and Patterns

The fun part about drawing groovy is decorating your art with colorful shapes and patterns that fill your art with personality! You can even invent your own patterns by combining basic shapes and patterns.

SHAPES

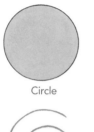
Circle

Oval

Dot

Spiral

Triangle

Diamond

Star

Half circle

Pointed half circle

Square

Rectangle

Simple flower

Leaf

Pointy leaf

Raindrop

Fat raindrop

Heart

Simple flower

PATTERNS

Dot

Broken line

Wave

Slanted humps

Loops

Jagged wave

Stripes and slanted stripes

Wavy line

Thinner wavy line

Zigzag

Crisscross

How to Draw a Pattern

A pattern is simply a shape, or a set of shapes, repeated in a row.
Here are several patterns created with multiple shapes.

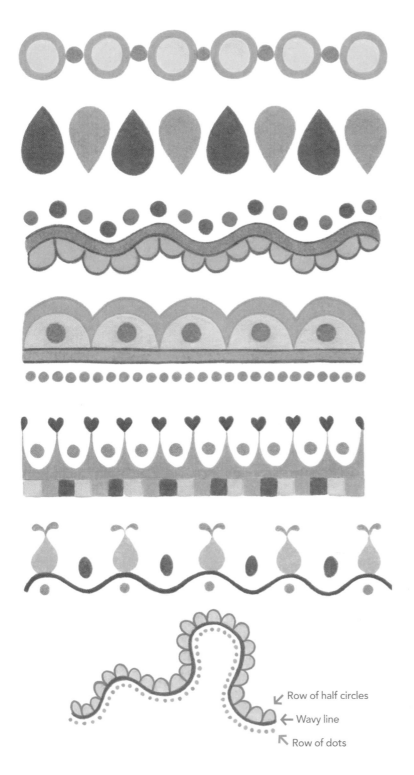

1 A row of circles, big and small.

2 A row of raindrops with every other raindrop drawn upside down.

3 Draw a purple wavy line, then add a row of dots on top and half circles below.

4 Draw a straight pink line and a row of dots underneath. On top of the pink line, draw yellow half circles with blue dots in the center, and then outline the yellow half circles with orange.

5 Now that you know how to draw patterns by repeating shapes, can you see how this pattern is made up of hearts, circles, waves and squares?

6 How many different shapes can you see in this pattern?

7 Patterns don't have to stay in a straight line—they can twist and curve, too!

← Row of half circles

← Wavy line

← Row of dots

Mandalas

Mandalas are fun, abstract designs based on circles, one inside another. Shapes and patterns are added, and the result is like an elegant doodle. Mandalas are created by many different cultures around the world.

 **1** Draw a dot with a circle around it. You can also trace a coin, cup or any round object to make a circle.

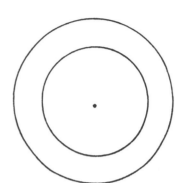 **2** Draw another circle around the circle.

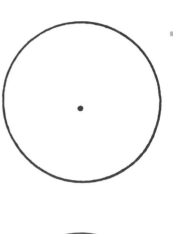 **3** Add shapes and patterns such as flower petals blooming out of the central dot.

 **4** Add half-circle petals around the inner circle.

 **5** Add pointy petals around the outer circle, then add small circles or dots inside each pointy petal.

6 Color it in!

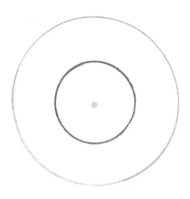

1 Draw a dot, then draw a circle around the dot, and then draw another larger circle around that.

2 Draw a design in the center and color it in.

3 Add patterns around the next circle and color in the background.

4 Draw dots around the outside edge of the circle.

5 Draw petals coming out of each dot.

Marker

Pen

Pen + colored pencil

Marker

Colored pencil

Flowers

Let's draw two different types of pretty flowers. All of the petals give us a chance to use a lot of colors! Once you get the hang of it, you can draw a bunch of flowers to make a garden or draw them inside a pot or vase.

1 Draw a yellow dot.

2 Draw a petal above the dot. Note the shape of the petal.

3 Draw 4 more matching petals around the yellow dot.

4 Draw a small rain-drop shape inside each petal.

5 Draw a pointy petal around each petal.

6 Color the inside shapes.

7 Color the rest of the petals.

8 Add a stem and leaves.

Pen + colored pencil

Colored pencil

1 Draw a circle.

2 Draw 4 short petals around the circle.

3 Draw 4 long petals around each of the short petals.

4 Draw 4 long petals in between the previous petals.

5 Draw 8 petals peeking out between each of the previous long petals.

6 Decorate the petals by adding details such as raindrops.

7 Draw a stem and leaves.

8 Color it in!

Colored pencil

Marker

Butterflies

Butterfly wings are perfect for adding shapes and patterns.
This cute butterfly has pretty wings decorated with flowers. What unique designs can you come up with?

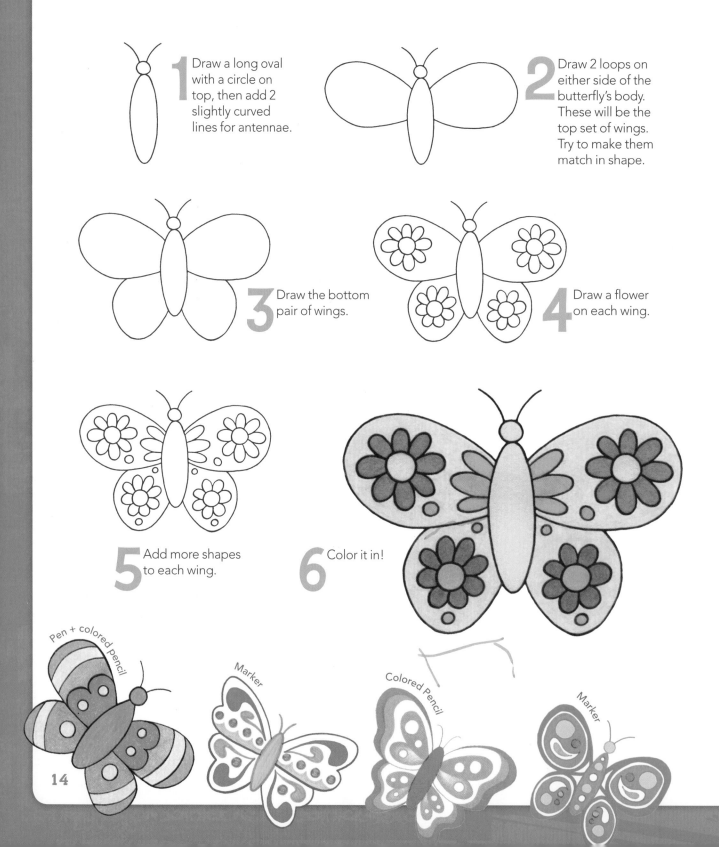

1 Draw a long oval with a circle on top, then add 2 slightly curved lines for antennae.

2 Draw 2 loops on either side of the butterfly's body. These will be the top set of wings. Try to make them match in shape.

3 Draw the bottom pair of wings.

4 Draw a flower on each wing.

5 Add more shapes to each wing.

6 Color it in!

Pen + colored pencil

Marker

Colored Pencil

Marker

1 Draw a long oval and color it in. At the top draw 2 slightly curved lines for antennae.

2 Draw a pair of top wings. Note the shape in the example. Try to make the wings match.

3 Draw a pair of bottom wings. Make them smaller than the top wings. Note the shape in the example.

4 Use different colors to draw shapes inside the wings such as the long raindrop shapes drawn here.

5 Add more shapes such as colored circles. You can also draw stars, hearts, loopy lines or wavy lines, anything you want!

6 Color in the background of the wings.

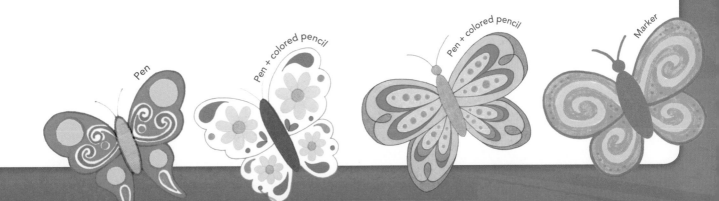

Pen

Pen + colored pencil

Pen + colored pencil

Marker

Birds

Let's draw a simple bird filled with patterns that give it personality!

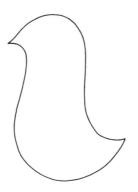

1 Starting from the top left of your paper, draw a curvy line that swoops down and then back up like the one you see here.

2 Go back to where you first began and draw a line that swoops up and then down like you see here. This is the bird's body.

3 Draw the bird's tail and 2 curved lines for feet.

4 Draw a line for a beak, a circle for an eye and a curved line for a wing.

5 Add shapes and patterns on the wing and tail.

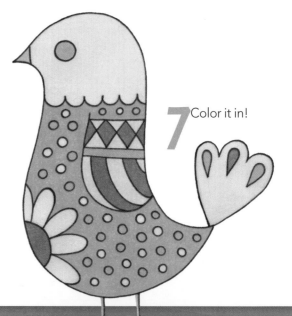

6 Decorate the rest of the bird's body with more shapes and patterns.

7 Color it in!

Marker

Colored pencil

Pen + colored pencil

Marker

Owls

Owls are fun to draw because of their wide-open eyes and fabulous feathers. They look great when you fill them with detail.

1 Draw a gently curving line that goes from left to right at the top of your paper.

2 Below the line, draw 2 large circles in the center that will be the owl's eyes. In between the owl's eyes, draw a V for a beak.

3 Draw a large *U*-shape that curves in slightly on each side near the top, connecting the curved line on top of the owl's eyes.

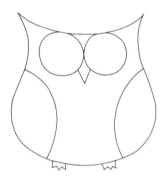

4 Draw a pair of feet and 2 curved lines for wings.

5 Decorate the eyes and wings with shapes and patterns like dots, flowers and waves.

7 Color it in!

6 Add more decorations to the owl's body. Let your imagination run wild!

Owls

Here is another way to draw an owl.
Think of all the designs you can add to its wings, chest and forehead.

1 Draw 2 straight lines that look like a wide V.

2 Draw a pair of eyes with the top of the eyes touching the bottom of the straight lines.

3 Draw a curved *U*-shaped line that goes from the top of one straight line to the top of the other straight line as you see here. This is the owl's body.

4 Draw a curve at the top for the owl's head and 2 curves inside the owl's body to make wings.

5 Draw the owl's feet and a narrow V for a beak.

6 Color in the owl with fun shapes and patterns!

Crayon on colored paper

Pen + colored pencil

Crayon

Marker

Pen + colored pencil

Pen + marker

21

Paisley

Paisley is a cute, fun shape that can be decorated in many ways.
It looks like a raindrop with a little twist at the top.

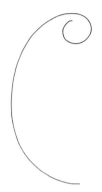

1 Draw a long, continuous curved line.

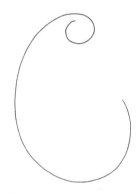

2 Without picking up your pencil, bring the curve back up.

3 Curve your line so it connects with the very beginning of your drawing. You've drawn a paisley outline!

4 Begin to decorate the inside of the paisley. Start with a raindrop shape in the big part of the paisley and a circle in the small part.

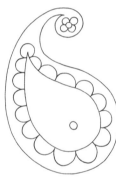

5 Add more patterns and shapes such as flower petals.

6 Draw a line around the outside edge of the paisley's big bulge.

7 Add more detail like lines, stripes, waves, flowers or whatever you can think of.

8 Color it in!

Pen + colored pencil

Pen + colored pencil

Pencil

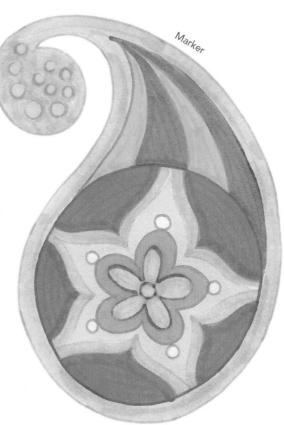

Marker

Hearts

This cute heart is decorated with colorful shapes and patterns.
Fill it with your own designs to make a fun surprise for someone you love!

 **1** Draw a heart.

 **2** Draw a heart around the heart.

 **3** Draw another heart around the heart.

 **4** Add decorations around the outside of the heart such as petals, loops, waves and dots.

 **5** Draw shapes inside the heart such as circles.

 **6** Add designs to the next layer of the heart.

 **7** Add more colors and patterns to create a fun, cheerful heart!

Pen + colored pencil

Marker

Marker

25

Shooting Stars

Shooting stars are a bright and colorful way to express your creativity.
Let your inner light shine!

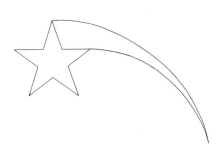

1 Use a pencil to draw a star.

2 Erase the lines inside the star.

3 Draw a small dot to the bottom right of your star. From the top of your star, draw a curved line that swoops down to the dot on the right. Then draw a similar curved line from the right tip of your star to the dot.

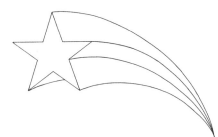

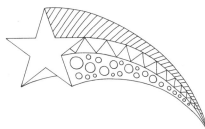

4 Draw more curved lines from the bottom tips of your star to the dot.

5 Draw patterns in between the lines you just drew. You can draw stripes, circles, waves, hearts, anything you want!

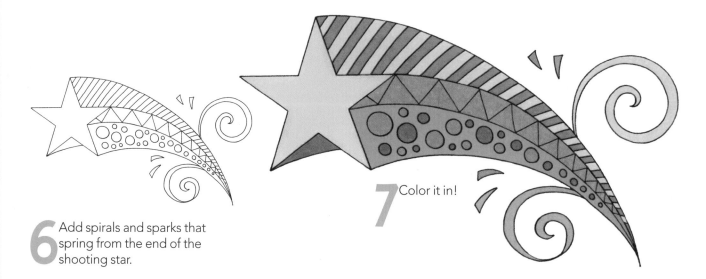

7 Color it in!

6 Add spirals and sparks that spring from the end of the shooting star.

Pen + colored pencil

Pen + colored pencil

Pen + marker

Pen + marker

Peace Signs

It's time to promote world peace! This groovy peace sign is full of flowers and smiles.
The steps drawn in blue should be drawn in pencil so you can erase them later.

1 Draw or trace a circle. Use a can, cup or any round object to make it perfectly round. Draw a vertical line in the middle of the circle.

2 Starting in the middle of the vertical line, draw a line that goes from the middle to the lower left side of the circle, then do the same thing on the right. This is how you draw a basic peace sign! Now we'll get even more groovy.

3 Draw a circle around the peace sign.

4 Inside the peace sign, draw 4 shapes that echo the shapes of the peace sign. For example, the bottom shapes will look like pie slices. Study the example to see the shapes.

5 Erase the lines you drew in steps 1 and 2. You will be left with the outline of a peace sign that is perfect for coloring and decorating!

6 In the center of the peace sign draw a smiley face. At each point where a straight line touches the circle, draw a flower.

7 Draw circles and flowers (or any other shapes and patterns) to fill in the rest of the peace sign.

8 Color it in!

Colored pencil

Pen + marker

Marker

Marker

Toadstools

A toadstool is a mushroom that is often associated with fairies and fairy tales. Draw a colorful mushroom that will attract a ring of dancing fairies!

 Draw a long line that loops down and back up again. This is the stem or stalk of the toadstool.

2 Draw a long oval with the top of the oval touching the top of the lines you drew in step 1. This is the inside of the toadstool.

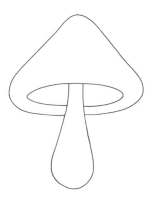

3 Starting below the oval, draw a bigger line that looks like a triangle with rounded edges. This part of the toadstool is called the *cap*.

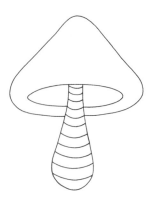

4 Add designs to the stem such as stripes, waves, loops and dots.

5 Add shapes and patterns to the outside of the toadstool. You can draw a bunch of flowers or circles, or you can do rows of different patterns as shown here.

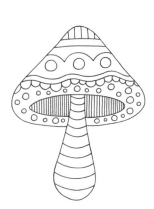

6 Draw vertical lines inside the toadstool. These are called the *gills*.

7 Color it in!

Colored pencil

Pen + colored pencil

Pen + marker

Marker

31

Russian Dolls

Russian nesting dolls usually come in a set of 5 or 6 hollow dolls, each one smaller than the next so they can be stacked inside each other. The dolls are decorated with pretty designs and patterns.

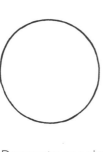 **1** Draw or trace a circle.

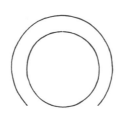 **2** Draw a circle around the first circle, but leave the bottom open.

 **3** On each of the edges of the outer circle, draw long, downward lines that curve outward and back in again.

 **4** Connect the 2 bottom points by drawing a long oval from point to point.

 **5** Draw the doll's face. Add hair, eyes and a mouth.

 **6** Draw patterns on the doll's body. In the center of the doll you can draw a mandala, a flower, a peace sign, a heart or anything you want!

 **7** Color it in!

Colored pencil

Pen + marker

Marker

Colored pencil

Baby Elephants

Elephants are fun to draw, with their big ears and tummies. Baby elephants don't yet have tusks, so they are easier to draw than grown-up elephants.

1 Start by drawing a long, gently sloping line. This will be the elephant's trunk.

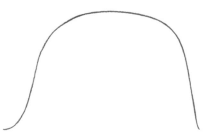

2 From the top of the line draw a hump for the elephant's back. Slope the line downward to create the elephant's back leg.

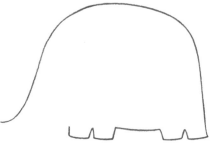

3 Draw 2 back feet, then the elephant's belly, then 2 front feet.

4 Draw the rest of the elephant's front leg and trunk.

5 Draw a circle for the eye, a curved line for the ear, and a tail. Decorate the ear and tail with shapes and colors.

6 Decorate the rest of the elephant's body with shapes such as stripes, circles, flowers, hearts, waves or anything you want! Color it in any way you like!

Pen + colored pencil

Marker

Pen + colored pencil

Colored pencil

Cat Heads

Cats are clever, mysterious creatures. Do you ever look in their eyes and wonder what they're thinking? Draw a cat whose fur reflects her personality!

1 Draw a wide *U*-shape with a slight point at the middle bottom.

2 Draw lines to complete each ear and connect the top of the head.

3 Draw triangles inside the cat's ears. Draw a nose and whiskers.

4 Draw the outlines of the cat's eyes.

5 Draw rounded slits for the cat's pupils. You can add little circles to look like reflections of light.

6 Color in the eyes.

7 Decorate the cat's head with shapes and patterns such as mandalas, hearts, dots and paisleys.

Pen + colored pencil

Pen

Pen + marker

Marker

Cat Bodies

Complete your cat by drawing its body.
Did you know that when a cat points her tail straight up in the air, she's saying hello?

1 Starting near the end of its left whiskers, draw a line underneath the cat's head that goes down and curves up to form a leg, and then down again and up to form another leg. Study the lines in the example image.

2 Draw a slightly sloping horizontal line from the edge of the cat's head, level with the top of its nose. Draw a similar line extending from the cat's front leg as shown in the example.

3 Draw the cat's tail.

4 Draw the cat's back legs.

5 Add patterns and shapes to the cat's body such as flowers, dots, waves and loops. Color it in!

Pen + marker

Marker

Pen + marker

Teapots

If you like tea parties, you'll enjoy drawing your own whimsical teapots!
You can draw them in all shapes and sizes—big and tall or short and small.

1 Draw 2 gently curved lines facing each other.

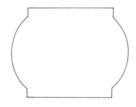

2 Draw the top and bottom of the teapot using vertical and horizontal lines as shown in the example.

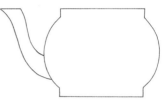

3 Draw the spout of the teapot.

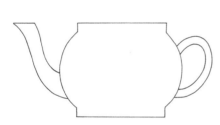

4 Draw the handle of the teapot.

5 Draw the lid of the teapot. In this teapot, the lid looks like a triangle with a circle at the top.

6 Add designs to the teapot such as stripes, loops and dots.

7 Color it in!

Marker

Pen + colored pencil

Pen + colored pencil

Marker

Teacups

Teacups come in many shapes and sizes. Let's draw a tall, elegant teacup and a round teacup decorated with pretty patterns.

1 Draw 2 parallel horizontal lines.

2 Draw 2 lines that curve slightly inward, connecting the top horizontal line to the bottom horizontal line.

3 Draw the base of the teacup as a horizontal line at the bottom.

4 Draw the handle of the teacup.

5 Decorate the teacup with colors and patterns.

6 Color in your drawing. What a pretty teacup!

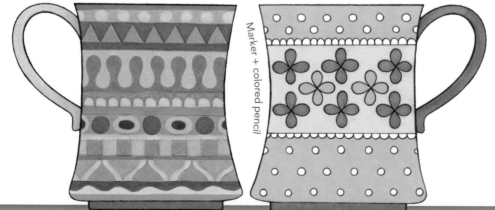

Marker + colored pencil

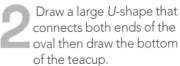

1 Draw a long, skinny, horizontal oval.

2 Draw a large *U*-shape that connects both ends of the oval then draw the bottom of the teacup.

3 Draw the curvy handle of the teacup.

4 Decorate your teacup with pretty designs.

5 Add more designs to make your teacup unique.

To shade the inside of the teacup, make it darker toward the left and right edges. You can layer colors such as blue and lavender as shown here.

6 Color it in!

Marker

Colored pencil, pen + marker

Fancy Hats

Draw a fancy hat to wear to your tea party! You can be as creative as you like and add flowers, stars and other whimsical designs to your hat.

1 Draw a horizontal oval.

2 Starting at the left and right edges of your oval, draw 2 long, gently curving lines downward, and then connect them at the bottom with a wide U-shape.

3 Draw the brim of the hat with the left and right sides curved upward.

4 Make your hat special by adding decorations such as flowers or stripes.

5 Add more decorations such as waves, raindrops, hearts and circles.

6 Add decorations to the brim of the hat.

7 Color it in!

Marker

Colored pencil

Marker + pen

Hot Air Balloons

The decorations on hot air balloons can be full of color and whimsy.
Draw and decorate a hot air balloon with your own unique designs.

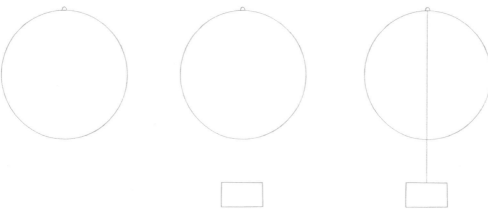

1 Draw a large circle with a very small upside-down U at the top center of the circle. This is the balloon.

2 Draw a rectangle underneath the circle. This is the basket.

3 Draw a straight vertical line from the top center of the circle to the top of the rectangle. This is one of the ropes that connect the balloon to the basket.

4 Draw straight lines from the sides of the balloon to the top left and right corners of the rectangle.

5 Draw 2 lines that start from the top center of the balloon and curve gently downward, ending on top of the basket.

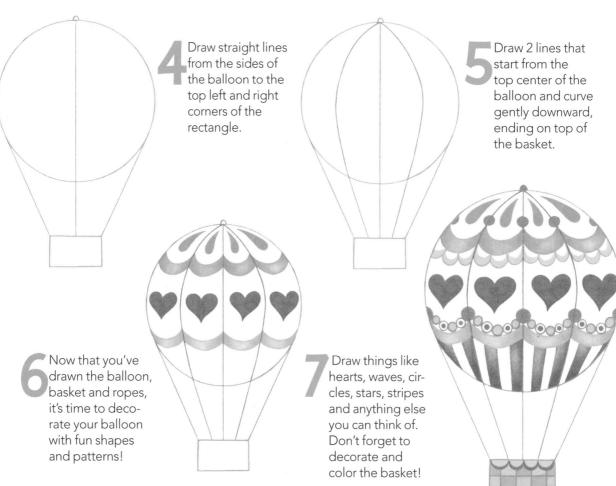

6 Now that you've drawn the balloon, basket and ropes, it's time to decorate your balloon with fun shapes and patterns!

7 Draw things like hearts, waves, circles, stars, stripes and anything else you can think of. Don't forget to decorate and color the basket!

Crayon + marker

Marker

Marker

Smiling Sun

This smiling sun has big eyes and groovy rays.
By doing some light shading around the edge of your sun, you can make it look 3-dimensional.

1 Draw a large circle. You can trace a cup, glass, lid, coaster or other round object.

2 Give your sun a face by drawing a pair of eyes, a curved line for a smile and 2 small circles at the edges of the smile to create rosy cheeks.

3 Color in the eyes and cheeks.

4 Color the sun yellow with orange shading around the edge of the circle.

5 Draw a ring of small petal shapes around the outside of the circle.

6 Draw the rays of the sun. You can draw the rays as lines, spikes, triangles or pointy waves as shown here.

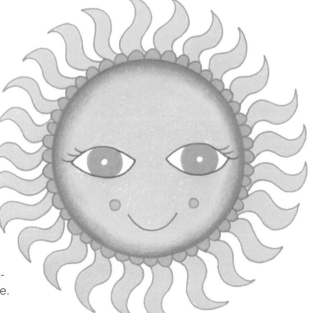

Colored pencil

Marker

Pen + marker

Marker

49

Mandala Flowers With Leaves

It's easy to turn mandalas (see page 10) into flowers. All you have to do is add a stem and leaves. Here are two ways to draw stems and cute leaves.

1 Draw a mandala and color it in.

2 At the bottom of the mandala, draw lines that curve gently downward to make a stem.

3 Draw a leaf. Repeat the same shape inside the leaf but smaller.

4 Draw a similar leaf on the opposite side of the stem.

5 Color it in using 2 different shades of green.

Alternate leaf colorings

1 Draw a mandala.

2 Starting at the bottom of the mandala, draw a long, straight green line going downward.

3 At the top of the green line, draw a green sideways raindrop shape on either side of the line with the points touching.

4 Draw another pair of raindrop shapes below your first pair.

5 Draw more pairs of leaves until you reach the bottom of the stem.

You can also add leaves to your mandala flowers by leaving out the stem and drawing the leaves directly touching the flower.

Flowers in Vases

Now that you know how to draw flowers and leaves, you can also draw pretty vases to put them in. Your vases can be tall and narrow or wide and bulky. It's up to you!

1 Near the middle of your paper, draw a short horizontal line. Near the bottom of your paper draw another horizontal line, a bit longer this time. Make sure to leave enough blank space at the top of your paper to draw flowers.

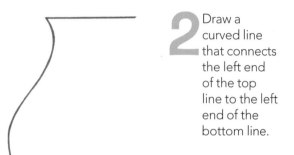

2 Draw a curved line that connects the left end of the top line to the left end of the bottom line.

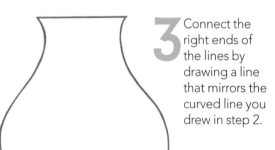

3 Connect the right ends of the lines by drawing a line that mirrors the curved line you drew in step 2.

4 Decorate your vase with patterns and shapes like hearts, stars, waves, dots, stripes and anything else you can think of.

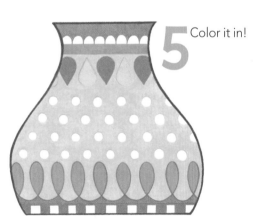

5 Color it in!

6 Add flowers and leaves.

Colored pencil

Pen + colored pencil

Pen + colored pencil

Pen + marker

53

Vines

If you like to doodle, you'll love drawing swirly vines. They're fun to draw on the edges of your notebook paper, or you can cover an entire sheet of paper with them.

1 Draw an elegant line with swirls and loops.

2 Draw lines that run parallel to the swirls and loops.

3 Color in the swirls and loops.

4 Draw patterns around the outside of the swirls and loops such as circles, petals and waves.

5 Add decorations such as dots, raindrops and small swirls.

6 Finish the vine by drawing flowers at each end. Color away!

Colored pencil + pen

Colored pencil

Marker + pen

Squiggle Abstracts

Abstract art is fun to create because you don't have to worry about making the art look like anything real. Instead, you focus on drawing shapes and patterns using any colors you want. Let the colors and patterns dance across your paper!

1 Draw a loopy squiggly line that overlaps itself in several places. Overlapping is important because it creates closed-in areas that you'll be decorating in the next steps.

2 Start drawing decorations on the outside and the inside of your loopy line.

3 Move from section to section drawing patterns inside the closed areas as well as outside the lines.

4 Draw things like dots, hearts, stripes, swirls, raindrops, waves, loops and flowers.

5 Experiment with different colors and shapes.

6 Continue adding decorations to your drawing. Try to make it feel balanced.

7 You are finished when you feel you are finished. There is no right or wrong when it comes to drawing squiggle abstracts!

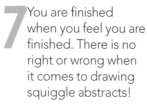

Colored pencil + pen

Pen

Marker

Mehendi

Mehendi refers to detailed decorations that are drawn on people's hands in India and other countries. Instead of drawing on your own hand, we'll draw mehendi-style designs on paper. Traditionally mehendi is drawn in one color, but you can use many different colors to express who you are!

1 Trace your hand onto a sheet of paper. Be sure to trace your wrist too.

2 In the center of the hand, draw a mandala or a flower or a heart or a star or any other image that you feel represents who you are.

3 Draw shapes and patterns on the fingers. Invent your own patterns by combining shapes like circles and raindrops as shown in this example.

4 Draw a pattern across the wrist.

5 Color it in!

Colored pencil

Marker

Colored pencil

Toadstool Houses

Earlier you learned to draw groovy toadstools.
Now let's turn those toadstools into colorful houses—the perfect homes for tiny gnomes!

1 On the bottom half of your paper draw a curved line that will be the stalk. This will be the ground floor of the house.

2 On top of the stalk draw the cap of the toadstool, which looks like a triangle with very rounded corners. This will be the roof and the top story of the house.

3 Draw a chimney on the cap and a front door on the stalk.

4 Draw windows on the cap.

5 Decorate the cap and the stalk with shapes and patterns. Add grass.

6 Color it in! You can also draw flowers and butterflies if you like.

Marker

Marker + pen

Colored pencil + pen

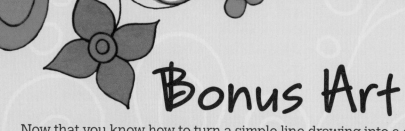

Bonus Art

Now that you know how to turn a simple line drawing into a groovy masterpiece, you can add colorful shapes and patterns to any drawing such as this funky sheep, sugar skull and pretty peacock!

about the Author

Thaneeya McArdle creates colorful art in a variety of styles, ranging from abstraction to photorealism. Her work hangs in private collections around the world, and can also be purchased on t-shirts, stickers, coloring books and more. Thaneeya created the popular art instruction site, Art-is-Fun.com, where she shares her love of art with fun lessons and detailed information on drawing, painting and mixed media. Her site has received over 16 million pageviews and counting. Thaneeya is also the founder of The Art Colony, an online community for artists of all skill levels. In addition to art, Thaneeya loves to travel and learn new things. You can see more of Thaneeya's artwork at thaneeya.com.

Acknowledgments

Thank you to the following: Sarah Laichas, my helpful editor; Brianna Scharstein, for designing such an awesome layout; Pam Wissman, who first approached me about this book; the members and moderators at The Art Colony for providing endless inspiration; and most of all a special thank you to my husband Marcus for EVERYTHING!

Dedication

To my groovy dad, for always encouraging my artistic endeavors.

Draw Groovy. Copyright © 2013 by Thaneeya McArdle. Manufactured in China. All rights reserved. No part of this book may be reproduced in any form or by any electronic or mechanical means including information storage and retrieval systems without permission in writing from the publisher, except by a reviewer who may quote brief passages in a review. Published by IMPACT Books, an imprint of F+W Media, Inc., 10151 Carver Road, Suite 200, Blue Ash, OH 45242. (800) 289-0963. First Edition.

 Other fine IMPACT Books are available from your favorite bookstore, art supply store or online supplier. Visit our website at fwmedia.com.

17 16   5   4

DISTRIBUTED IN CANADA BY FRASER DIRECT
100 Armstrong Avenue
Georgetown, ON, Canada L7G 5S4
Tel: (905) 877-4411

DISTRIBUTED IN THE U.K. AND EUROPE
BY F&W MEDIA INTERNATIONAL, LTD
Brunel House, Forde Close, Newton Abbot, TQ12 4PU, UK
Tel: (+44) 1626 323200, Fax: (+44) 1626 323319
Email: enquiries@fwmedia.com

DISTRIBUTED IN AUSTRALIA BY CAPRICORN LINK
P.O. Box 704, S. Windsor NSW, 2756 Australia
Tel: (02) 4560 1600; Fax: (02) 4577 5288
Email: books@capricornlink.com.au

ISBN 13: 978-1-4403-2216-7

Edited by Sarah Laichas
Designed by Brianna Scharstein
Production coordinated by Mark Griffin

✱ BONUS MATERIAL

Visit impact-books.com/drawgroovy to download a free bonus demonstration of a happy snail!